Why Recycle?

Contents

written by Julie Ellis

Recycling means using something again.
Sometimes things that cost a lot of money
can be used again in a different way.

When things are no longer useful, we often throw them away, and buy new ones. Many people don't think about recycling things.

Why should we recycle things when we stop using them?
We wonder what use they would be to anyone else.
But there are good reasons for recycling.

4

We can make money, save money, help other people, and help the environment. New things can be made from old stuff. It can also be fun to recycle.

One reason to recycle is that you can make money from things you don't want. Some people have a sale at their home. Others use the Internet or the newspaper to sell things. Some old things are valuable because they were made so long ago that there are not many left.

Good pieces of old furniture, called antiques, are easy to sell. People called collectors pay a lot of money for old things that they want, like books, clocks, teaspoons, and bottles.

You can save money by buying second-hand things.
They are not new, but they are often still good.
If you want more sports gear or games, or even
a bike, these often cost much less money if you
buy them second-hand.

8

Some things like furniture and clocks were made to last a long time. Special stores sell good things that don't cost very much because somebody has used them before.

Another good reason to recycle is to help the environment. Do you know that thousands of things are made from trees? If things like wood, cardboard, and paper are recycled, we won't have to cut down so many trees to make more.

It is important to recycle things like mobile phones, television sets, and microwaves. If they still work, they can be given to people who will use them. If they don't work, their parts can be used again.

Shoes, glasses, and books can be collected second-hand and sent to where they are needed. Even old clothes are useful. Buttons are reused, while the oldest clothes are turned into cleaning rags.

People say, "One person's junk is another person's treasure." When things are being recycled, they often need to be collected, sorted, mended, and cleaned before they can be used again.

All towns and cities have special places to take
paper, plastic, cans, and glass. In most places,
trucks are sent to collect things for recycling.
You can find out from the Internet or your
council where to send things you don't need.

R
PLEAS
RECYCL
ALUMINUM ONLY
PLASTIC ONLY
TIN ONLY
ALUMINUM
RECYCLING
PLASTIC
RECYCLING
TIN
RECYCLING

14

There are many different kinds of plastic, and most of them can't be mixed together. Every plastic container has a number to show which kind it is, so that people know which pieces can be recycled.

recycling station

Recycling can be fun! Make your own artwork and toys from junk. Try making a kite from plastic, string, and sticks. Could you make a bird feeder or a wind chime? What else?